HOME   AWAY

Soccer School

By Deborah Lock

Penguin
Random
House

Series Editor Deborah Lock
Project Editor Camilla Gersh
Editor Nandini Gupta
Designer Emma Hobson
Art Editor Jyotsna Julka
Managing Editor Soma B. Chowdhury
Managing Art Editor Ahlawat Gunjan
Art Director Martin Wilson
Senior Producer, Pre-production Ben Marcus
Senior DTP Designer Sachin Singh
DTP Designers Anita Yadav, Syed Md. Farhan
Picture Researcher Surya Sarangi

Reading Consultant
Linda B. Gambrell, Ph.D.

First American Edition, 2015
Published in the United States by DK Publishing
1745 Broadway, 20th Floor, New York, NY 10019

Copyright © 2015 Dorling Kindersley Limited.
A Penguin Random House Company
22 10 9 8 7 6 5
007—271678—September/15

A catalog record for this book is available from the Library of Congress.
ISBN: 978-1-4654-3583-5 (Paperback)
ISBN: 978-1-4654-3582-8 (Hardcover)

Printed and bound in China

DK books are available at special discounts when purchased in bulk for sales promotions, premiums,
fund-raising, or educational use. For details, contact: DK Publishing Special Markets,
1745 Broadway, 20th Floor, New York, NY 10019
SpecialSales@dk.com

The publisher would like to thank the following for their kind permission to reproduce their photographs:
(Key: a-above; b-below/bottom; c-center; f-far; l-left; r-right; t-top)
14–15 Getty Images: Thomas Barwick / Digital Vision.
34 Corbis: Colorsport (crb). **Getty Images:** AFP / Stringer (clb). **35 Corbis:** Laurent Baheux /
TempSport (clb); Jerry Cooke (crb). **41 Alamy Images:** IS098U7WR / Image Source.
43 Getty Images: Christian MartA-nez Kempin / E+. **45 Corbis:** Dario Secen / Lumi Images.
53 Getty Images: Andersen Ross / Digital Vision. **54–55 Getty Images:** Tim Macpherson / Cultura.
57 Alamy Images: Allstar Picture Library (l).
Jacket images: *Front:* **Getty Images:** Image Source.
All other images © Dorling Kindersley
For further information see: www.dkimages.com

A WORLD OF IDEAS:
SEE ALL THERE IS TO KNOW

www.dk.com

Contents

Chapter 1
History

Soccer has become one of the most popular sports in the world. Millions of people watch matches on television. Top teams have a huge following of fans. Children around the world play the game wherever and whenever they can.

Ball-kicking games have existed since ancient times. In China and other Eastern countries, the games were part of military training and ceremonies. In Europe, the games were more a crazy free-for-all. **Opposing** teams would play through towns or in squares. People found that an inflated animal's bladder covered in leather made a light, bouncy ball. The design is still used today but made from other materials.

The rules of the modern game of soccer were set out in 1863 by the first soccer **association** in Britain. The game spread quickly to other countries. In 1904, the Fédération Internationale de Football Association (FIFA) was formed. More than 200 countries have now joined.

The FIFA World Cup is one of the world's greatest sporting events. Since 1930, the event has been held every four years.

Soccer is popular because it has simple rules and little equipment is needed to play. Yet, the game tests players' speed, agility, and brave spirit.

When buying soccer equipment, there are three points to keep in mind. Each piece should be comfortable, hard-wearing, and lightweight.

The most important items are the shoes. They are designed to help players use the inside and outside of their feet. The softer the leather, the easier it is to feel the ball. The studs on the base of the shoes vary depending on the type of surface. Flat rubber studs are ideal for hard ground, aluminum studs are for wet and slippery ground, and nylon studs are for soft but firm ground. If playing on artificial grass, tiny molded studs give the best grip.

THE FIELD

Soccer is played on a flat, rectangular field. It can be made of real grass or artificial grass like AstroTurf.

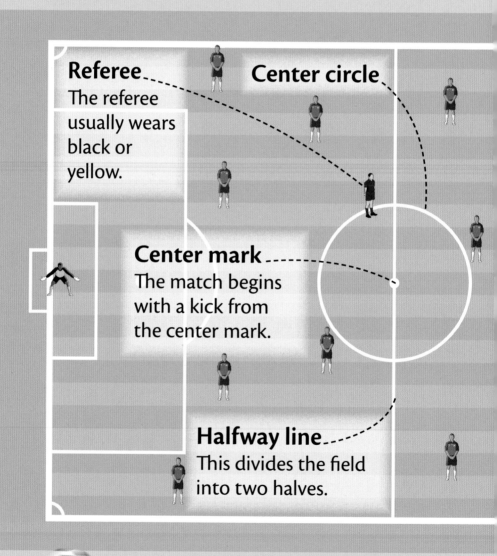

Referee
The referee usually wears black or yellow.

Center circle

Center mark
The match begins with a kick from the center mark.

Halfway line
This divides the field into two halves.

Corner arc
Corner kicks are
taken from here.

Penalty area
If a player is **fouled**
in this box, his team
will be allowed to
take a penalty kick.

Goal
If the ball crosses
the goal line between
the goal posts, a goal
is scored.

Goal area
The goalie takes goal
kicks from here when
the ball crosses
the goal line without
scoring a goal.

Penalty spot
Penalty kicks are
taken from here.

Chapter 2
Practice

Professional soccer players reached the top by practicing and perfecting their skills. Joining a club or team is the best way to start out. Today, players can start at a very young age.

A coach is the person who runs the training sessions. The players' fitness and skills are very important. The coach decides what the team needs to work on so that the players perform their best in a match. During the match, the coach watches the players and then tells them what they can learn from their game.

Training sessions should always begin with a warm up. This helps the players get their bodies ready for activity. Walking, jogging, backward skipping, and sideways running gets the heart to beat quicker. These warm ups also help the players' muscles move and get stronger.

For older players, some easy stretches loosen up parts of the body that will be used in training. Lifting knees high or taking large steps in a lunge while walking help flex the hips and the lower legs.

At the end of a training session, it is important to cool down with some easy, gentle moves.

Ball control is the key to soccer success. Training involves practicing ways to control and use the ball in all situations. Players can receive a ball at any height and at any speed. They need to know how to use their feet, thigh, chest, or head to bring the ball under control quickly. Balance is the key.

Sometimes, the ball needs to be stopped dead. To do this, the ball is trapped under the sole of a foot. If the ball comes to a player at a higher level, the inside of one foot is raised to receive it. The longer the foot stays in contact with the ball, the more control the player has. A steady supporting leg, slightly bent, helps keep balance. Players also balance themselves with their arms. The secret of perfect control is to keep the body turned toward the ball.

Players first learn the skill of controlling the ball standing still. But for a match, players need to learn to do this on the move.

Dribbling is the ultimate skill of close control of the ball. Players run with the ball close to their feet, pushing it forward with quick, sharp kicks. Both the inside and the outside of one foot is used in turn so that the direction of the ball can be changed quickly. When dribbling, the ball must look as if it is tied to a player's shoelaces.

> **"Learn to dribble and to think, all at the same time."**
>
> *Geoff Hurst, England's hat trick hero of the 1966 World Cup*

During training sessions, players practice and practice the key footwork skills. Repeating moves helps form a rhythm. Practicing also helps speed up the moves.

LEARN THE RAÍ FLICK

1 Head toward the defender with the ball and let the ball roll a bit. Then hop on the ball and grip it by the sides.

2 Jump and lift the ball with your feet behind you. Flick the ball with your heel, up and over your shoulder and the defender.

20

This is a great trick for getting around defenders.

3 Run on and get ready for the ball to drop. That will be your moment to strike!

Chapter 3
Key Skills

HOME   AWAY

Soccer is a team game. It is about eleven players, working together to gain and keep possession of the ball to be able to score a goal. Passing, dribbling, kicking, heading, **tackling**, and shooting are some of the key skills to master. In a match, players need to judge a situation clearly, and quickly decide what skill is best to use.

Passing gets the ball to teammates so that they can receive it and control it. Players should always look for opportunities to move into spaces to pick up and return passes.

There are different types of passes. The push pass is the most accurate because the large area of the inside part of the foot comes into contact with the ball. The middle strike on the ball keeps it low. The follow-through of the foot controls the speed and the direction the ball travels.

The backheel pass is a quick, short-range kick to a teammate behind. This is a surprise move to

avoid a tackle. The lofted pass is a powerful backswing kick to get the ball to a teammate farther up the field. The bottom of the ball is kicked with the instep of the foot.

The wall pass is also known as the "one-two." Two players pass the ball quickly to each other to get around an opposing player. After using a push pass to a teammate, the player runs on, ready to receive the return pass. The pass is like a ball "bouncing" back off a wall.

> **"Knowing when to dribble, when to pass—this is the true skill."**
>
> *Roberto Baggio, Italian team, one of the top goalscorers in the 1994 World Cup*

If players have a lot of space in front of them, choosing to run with the ball can cause chaos for the opposing team. However, this is risky and too often players lose the ball. Players should always keep looking up to decide on their next move.

There are many different ways to direct a soccer ball. Players can use the full instep of a foot, the inside or outside of a foot, their toes, or their heels. The ball can be pushed, chipped, **volleyed**, or kicked a long way. Players need to have the skills to do these moves with each foot. They also need to know how to keep their balance. The position of the head and supporting leg, the turn of the body, and the spread of the arms will affect the movement of the ball. For example, leaning slightly backward as the ball is kicked will lift it.

All soccer players need to learn the skill of tackling. The aim is to gain possession of the ball by making the player on

the opposing team lose the ball. The two positions for a tackle are from the front, facing each other, or from one side in a diagonal. A block tackle is when both players have an equal chance of winning the ball. Players keep their eyes on the ball and bend their knees to strengthen the tackle.

A slide tackle is used to clear the ball away. Players slide down low, using the full weight of the body. Timing the slide needs to be perfect.

Goalkeepers have another set of skills to master. They have to be able to judge where the ball is going and move into position quickly. For a ground shot, they

kneel behind the incoming ball ready to scoop it into the chest. For a high shot, hands are slightly apart with fingers and thumbs spread in a W-shape behind the ball for a clean catch. Slightly bent arms take the shock to cut the speed of the ball. Goalkeepers also leap and dive to reach the ball, even punching it out of the way if a clean catch is not possible.

Goalkeepers do much more than just stop shots going into the net. Once the ball is in their hands, they are ready to throw it quickly overarm back up the field or underarm to a teammate nearby.

HOW TO SCORE A PENALTY

It requires nerves of steel to take a good penalty. Here is how the greats do it.

QUICKSTART GUIDE

1 PRACTICE

Practice taking penalties in an open net first. Then practice with a goalkeeper.

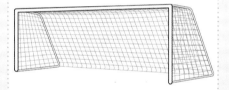

2 AIM

The corners are the hardest areas for the goalkeeper to reach. Aim for those areas.

3 MAKE A PLAN

When you are taking a penalty in a match, decide where you want to hit the kick, and stick to that plan.

4 GIVE NO CLUES

Try not to give the goalkeeper any clues. Aim away from where you are actually going to kick.

5 CONTROL

Do not blast the ball when you kick it. You will have less control over the shot.

6 BE READY FOR A REBOUND

If the goalkeeper saves, be ready for any possible rebounds. You can score even if you miss the first shot!

KEY PLAYERS

GOALKEEPER

The goalkeeper protects the goal and can use his or her hands to catch the ball.

AGILITY ★★★★★
TACKLING ★★
PASSING ★★★
SHOOTING ★

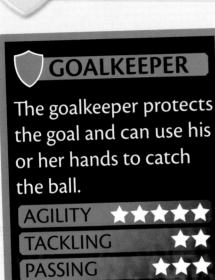

Positions: goalkeeper only.

DEFENDER

A defender tries to stop the opposition attacking and scoring.

AGILITY ★★
TACKLING ★★★★★
PASSING ★★★
SHOOTING ★

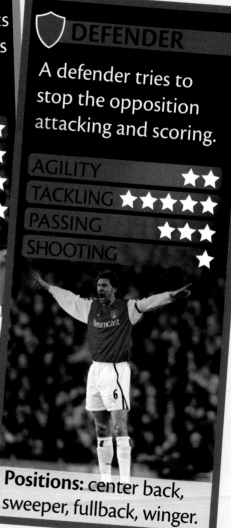

Positions: center back, sweeper, fullback, winger.

The 11 players on a team are grouped into positions that play special roles during a match.

FORWARD

An attacker scores goals and helps the midfielders.

AGILITY	★★★
TACKLING	★★
PASSING	★★★
SHOOTING	★★★★★

Positions: center forward, striker, second striker, outside forward, winger.

MIDFIELDER

A midfielder supports the defense and creates chances to attack.

AGILITY	★★★
TACKLING	★★★
PASSING	★★★★★
SHOOTING	★★

Positions: center, defensive, attacking, wide.

Chapter 4
Match

A soccer match is played between two teams of 11 players. They compete to score the most goals. Goals are scored by putting the ball into the opposing team's goal. The game is divided into two halves. Each half lasts 45 minutes. The team that wins the coin toss chooses which goal to attack in the first half. The other team takes the kickoff to start the match.

The game seems simple, but there are rules to make it run smoothly. A referee and at least two assistants make sure the rules are followed and the match is played fairly. They also act as timekeepers.

The team's coach decides how the players arrange themselves on the field. The number of attackers, midfielders, and defenders will depend on the team's tactics for the match.

The attackers are the strong goal scorers. They also need to run into good positions to receive passes and crosses.

The defenders are the strong tacklers. Their job is to stop the opposing team from gaining the ball. They stay close to the attackers on the other team, marking them to stop them from passing, shooting, or getting the ball.

The midfielders swap between playing in defense or on the attack. They know when to do a short pass to a nearby teammate or a long pass upfield.

The halftime break lasts 15 minutes in a professional soccer match. This break gives the players a chance to have a drink. It also gives the coach the chance to speak to them about their play. Are the tactics working against the opposing players? What is the team doing well? Are there changes that need to be made?

In the second half, the teams change ends and the team that won the toss kicks off.

> **"Make the ball your friend."**
>
> *Pelé, the legendary Brazilian striker. He was a member of the teams that won the World Cup in 1958, 1962, and 1970.*

The referee and assistants make the decision if a player commits a foul. A foul is when a player has not played fair. Tripping, charging, or pulling a player or touching the ball are types of fouls. A free kick is given to the opposite team. If the foul is in the penalty area, a shot at the goal is taken from the penalty spot with only the goalkeeper to beat.

The coach can swap players if one gets injured or tired. Players who are swapped out cannot return to the field though.

Throughout the match, the referee keeps note of time lost for injuries or stoppages. This time is then added on to the end of each half.

43

Fans cheer wildly, eager for their team to score. Goals can be scored from well-planned shots or from spotting a great chance. A soccer goal is 8 yards (7.3 meters) wide and 8 feet (2.4 meters) high, and positioned at the center of the goal line.

Good strikers have a range of shooting skills and shoot at every chance. They also know the goal so well that they don't even need to look at it before making a shot. However, when a goal is scored, it is often due to a team effort. No wonder everyone goes wild!

THE REFEREE

The referee has full authority during a match. He or she uses a set of official signals to show decisions made.

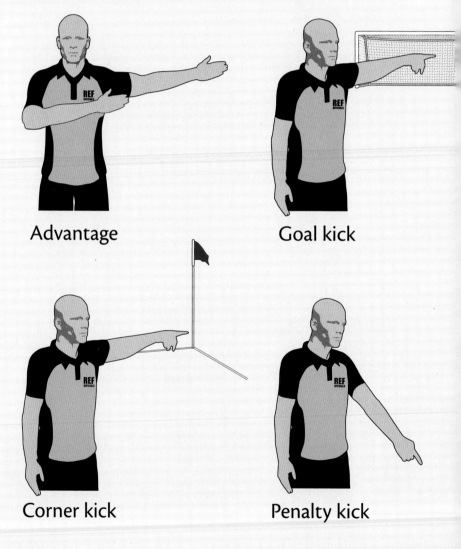

Advantage

Goal kick

Corner kick

Penalty kick

Red card
(sending off)

Yellow card
(caution)

Direct
free kick

Indirect
free kick

FORMATIONS

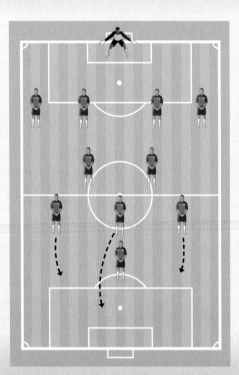

4-2-3-1

In this formation, two midfielders are used in front of the defense to maintain control of the midfield and the ball. This formation provides good defense but also allows for attacking.

4-4-2

In a 4-4-2 formation, the two wide midfielders move up to the goal line in attack but protect the wide defenders too. This formation is good for attacking and defending.

An important part of teamwork is playing in formation. Here are some of the most common formations.

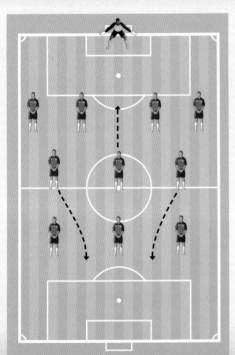

4-3-3

In this attacking formation, two midfielders push forward. The other midfielder drops back to help defense.

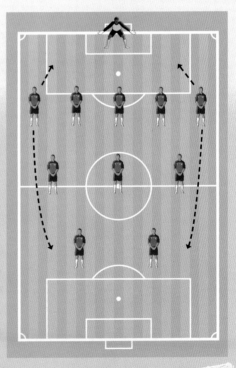

5-3-2

In this formation, the wide players (wingbacks) help with defense and attack. This formation can be very strong on defense.

49

Chapter 5
Turn Pro

So you want to become a professional soccer player? Reaching the top has many rewards—the best is to actually play the game you love. However, very, very few players make it to the top despite all the very hard practice, skills, and talent.

When you join a club, there are opportunities to play in competitions. Teams can be a mix of boys and girls at certain ages. Small side soccer games with four to seven players per side are fast and give plenty of chances to get the ball. The matches are played on half-size fields and often with a smaller, lighter ball.

For older players, matches are played between all-male or all-female teams. There are junior competitions for under-17s and youth competitions for under-21s.

In many countries, although less used in the US, there is a scouting system. A person goes to local matches to scout for talent, looking for gifted young players. Some are looking for players as young as six years old to join their club to train and develop.

Once spotted by a club **scout**, players are invited to the club for a trial. The club not only looks at how the players perform with a ball but also check the players' health and fitness. They also look out for how the players think, feel, and behave.

Young players who are successful go to the club's training school.

The training is tough and only a few players make it through. They are asked to stay on with the club. They play in the reserves and nursery teams before finally reaching their dream of becoming a top soccer player.

Soccer is a game to be enjoyed for the rest of your life as a player and a supporter. Whatever your level of play, skills can always be practiced and improved. Around the world, there is always a ball being kicked around in a city park, a dusty sidestreet, a school playground, or a remote village. Soccer has been called "the beautiful game" because it is so simple and it can be played and enjoyed everywhere.

Which team would you like to play for or support?

SOCCER BLOG

HOW THE PROS TURN PRO

- First, you'll need to get spotted. Join your school's team or a local club. Most professional clubs send scouts out to these games. Scouts travel around looking for talented young players.

- Getting noticed is not just about always playing at your best. Scouts are also looking for players who are passionate and work well with teammates.

- Between the ages of 9 and 16, selected players train several times a week and must also attend regular school. At 16, the club will decide which of its academy players can advance to its youth training program. This is very **competitive**.

- After the youth training program, players might move on to the reserves and then an under-21 team. Players are allowed to sign a contract at 17, but most will have to wait until they are 19.

56

X

HOME | BLOG | COACHING

MUST-READ

 What makes a great soccer stadium? Read about Wembley Stadium in the UK.

RECENT POSTS

Find out more about how to turn pro by reading David Beckham's amazing story, from his early days at Manchester United to becoming England captain.

Soccer Fun Facts

On average, each player in a match has the ball for only three minutes—the time it takes to boil an egg!

The first person to score from a penalty in a World Cup final was Johan Neeskens for Holland in 1974.

Luis Chilavert, goalkeeper for Paraguay, rushed out of his goal and scored for his team in a match against Argentina in 1998. The final score was 1–1.

Only seven different countries have been World Cup champions, although there have been 18 finals.

Pelé scored 1,283 goals in his professional career.

Soccer Quiz

1. In what year were the first rules of soccer set out?

2. How many players make a team in soccer?

3. What colors does the referee usually wear?

4. A match begins with a kick from which spot?

5. Which formation has two midfielders moving forward and one dropping back?

Answers on page 61.

Glossary

association
organized group of people who share the same interest

competitive
always trying to win

dribbling
running with the ball and pushing it with quick kicks

foul
when a player breaks the rules by kicking, tripping, or pushing another player

opposing
in competition with another team or person

penalty kick
shot from the penalty spot taken after a foul in the penalty area

professional
paid for doing a specific activity

scout
person who looks for talented new players for a club

tackling
stopping the player with the ball and removing the ball with the feet

volley
kick the ball before it touches the ground

Index

Answers to the Soccer Quiz:

1. 1863; **2.** 11; **3.** Black or yellow;
4. Center mark; **5.** 4-3-3.

Guide for Parents

DK Readers is a four-level interactive reading adventure series for children, developing the habit of reading widely for both pleasure and information. These books have an exciting main narrative interspersed with a range of reading genres to suit your child's reading ability, as required by the Common Core State Standards. Each book is designed to develop your child's reading skills, fluency, grammar awareness, and comprehension in order to build confidence and engagement when reading.

Ready for a *Reading Alone* book

YOUR CHILD SHOULD

- be able to read most words without needing to stop and break them down into sound parts.
- read smoothly, in phrases and with expression. By this level, your child will be mostly reading silently.
- self-correct when some word or sentence doesn't sound right.

A VALUABLE AND SHARED READING EXPERIENCE

For some children, text reading, particularly nonfiction, requires much effort, but adult participation can make this both fun and easier. So here are a few tips on how to use this book with your child.

TIP 1 Check out the contents together before your child begins:

- invite your child to check the blurb, contents page, and layout of the book and comment on it.
- ask your child to make predictions about the story.
- talk about the information your child might want to find out.

TIP 2 Encourage fluent and flexible reading:

- support your child to read in fluent, expressive phrases, making full use of punctuation and thinking about the meaning.

- encourage your child to slow down and check information where appropriate.

TIP 3 Indicators that your child is reading for meaning:

- your child will be responding to the text if he/she is self-correcting and varying his/her voice.
- your child will want to talk about what he/she is reading or is eager to turn the page to find out what will happen next.

TIP 4 Share and discuss:

- encourage your child to recall specific details after each chapter.
- provide opportunities for your child to pick out interesting words and discuss what they mean.
- discuss how the author captures the reader's interest, or how effective the nonfiction layouts are.
- ask questions about the text. These help develop comprehension skills and awareness of the language used.

A FEW ADDITIONAL TIPS

- Read to your child regularly to demonstrate fluency, phrasing, and expression; to find out or check information; and for sharing enjoyment.
- Encourage your child to reread favorite texts to increase reading confidence and fluency.
- Check that your child is reading a range of different types of material, such as poems, jokes, and following instructions.

Series consultant, **Dr. Linda Gambrell**, Distinguished Professor of Education at Clemson University, has served as President of the National Reading Conference, the College Reading Association, and the International Reading Association. She is also reading consultant for the **DK Adventures**.

Have you read these other great books from DK?

Meet the sharks who live on the reef or come passing through.

Join David on an amazing trip to meet elephants in Asia and Africa.

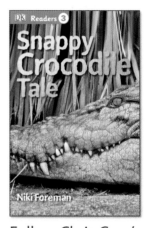

Follow Chris Croc's adventures from a baby to a mighty king of the river.

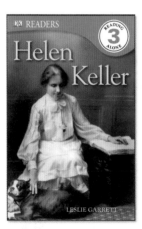

Read about the remarkable story of the deaf-blind girl who achieved great things.

Design and test a rocket for a spying mission. Try out some experiments at home.

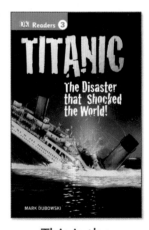

This is the incredible true story of the "unsinkable" ship that sank.